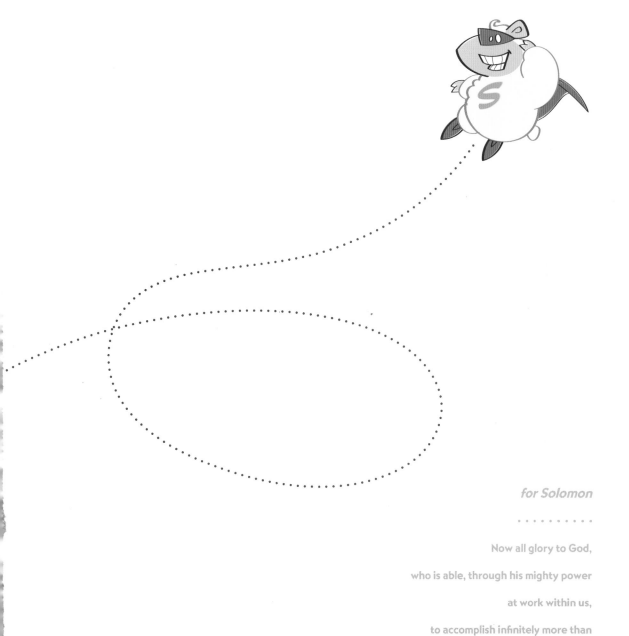

for Solomon

. . . .

Now all glory to God,

who is able, through his mighty power

at work within us,

to accomplish infinitely more than

we might ask or think.

EPHESIANS 3:20

Visit Tyndale's exciting Web site for kids at www.tyndale.com/kids.

TYNDALE is a registered trademark of Tyndale House Publishers, Inc.

The Tyndale Kids logo is a trademark of Tyndale House Publishers, Inc.

Rumble! Zap! Pow! Mighty Stories of God

Designed by Ron Kaufmann

Production by Ruth Berg

Edited by Stephanie Voiland

Published in association with the literary agency of Books & Such, 4788 Carissa Ave., Santa Rosa, CA 95406-7953.

Scripture quotations are taken from the Holy Bible, New Living Translation, copyright © 1996, 2004, 2007 by Tyndale House Foundation. Used by permission of Tyndale House Publishers, Inc., Carol Stream, Illinois 60188. All rights reserved.

For manufacturing information regarding this product, please call 1-800-323-9400.

Library of Congress Cataloging-in-Publication Data

Stortz, Diane M.
    Rumble! zap! pow! : mighty stories of God / Diane Stortz ; [illustrated by] Luke Daab.
      p. cm.
    ISBN 978-1-4143-3211-6 (hc)
 1. Bible stories, English. I. Title.
    BS551.3.S768 2010
    220.9′505--dc22
                     2009054158

Printed in China

16   15   14   13   12   11   10

7   6   5   4   3   2   1

RUMBLE! ZAP! POW!

MIGHTY STORIES OF GOD

WRITTEN BY
Diane Stortz

ILLUSTRATED BY
Luke Daab

TYNDALE KIDS

Tyndale House Publishers, Inc.
CAROL STREAM, ILLINOIS

Contents

NEW TESTAMENT STORIES

Introduction

The stories in this book show God's strong love, goodness, and power. What better stories for energetic preschoolers than accounts from the Bible filled with action, adventure, and the assurance that we can always trust our mighty God?

These short, action-filled stories are perfect for active young children. Along with colorful, comic-book-style illustrations, each story includes the three common elements (right): Mighty Thought, Power Words, and Activity.

Super Sheep is ready to guide you through the book. He's super because he knows our mighty God! So turn the page and let's . . .

a Mighty Thought to tell kids who God is and what he does

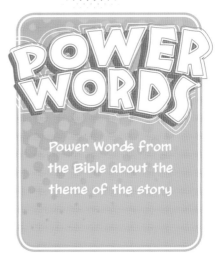

Power Words from the Bible about the theme of the story

ACTIVITY

an Activity to extend children's learning through movement and doing

Seven Super Days

GENESIS 1-2

MIGHTY THOUGHT

God made the world.

In the beginning, out of nothing, God made everything.

Day 1

God said...

LIGHT!

The dark ran away. God called the light *day*, and he called the dark *night*.

Day 2

SPACE!

Blue sky sparkled way up high.

Day 3

DRY GROUND!

The land rose up, with seas all around.

Day **6**

ANIMALS OF ALL KINDS!

Everything God made was good.

Now for the best part. People! They will live on the earth and take care of it.

God made a man named Adam and a woman named Eve.

Day **7**

YES, IT'S VERY GOOD!

God rested.

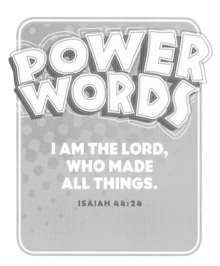

POWER WORDS

I AM THE LORD, WHO MADE ALL THINGS.

ISAIAH 44:24

ACTIVITY

Find your crayons or markers. Get these colors: red, blue, green, yellow, and purple. In your yard or at the park, match the colors of your crayons to the colors of God's beautiful world.

Delicious?

GENESIS 3

MIGHTY THOUGHT

God knows what's best.

Adam and Eve lived in a garden. A slithery snake asked Eve...

Feeling hungry?

Try some fruit from the tree of knowing good and evil.

God told us not to.

The fruit won't hurt you. You'll be wise like God, that's all.

...the snake lied.

God told the snake...

From now on, you will crawl on your belly.

Then God told Adam and Eve...

You ate the fruit. You cannot live forever. You must leave the garden.

God sent mighty angels and a fiery sword to guard the garden.

Someday, God promised, someone would come to make things right again.

POWER WORDS

FOLLOW ALL HIS WAYS.

1 KINGS 2:3

ACTIVITY

With some friends and a grown-up, play Simon Says. Choose one person to be Simon. Simon gives commands that start with "Simon says," like "Simon says rub your tummy" or "Simon says hop on one foot." But sometimes Simon does not say "Simon says" when he or she gives a command.

If a command begins with "Simon says," obey the command or you'll be out. But if the command does not begin with "Simon says," don't do it or you'll be out. Listen closely!

Afloat on a Boat

GENESIS 6-7

MIGHTY THOUGHT

God does what he says.

God said...

Noah, I'm sending a flood. Build a big boat. I'll keep you safe.

Noah believed God. He got busy.

ZOOMFA

ZOOMFA

Noah and his sons cut wood.

They fit the pieces together to make the boat.

TAP, TAP! BAM, BAM!

They coated the boat with tar so it would float.

And Mrs. Noah gathered food to take on board.

HA-HA!

TEE-HEE!

Silly old Noah. What's he doing?

How can the earth flood? We've never even seen rain.

People laughed at Noah while he worked.

Noah kept on building. And when the boat was done...

...two by two, animals of every kind came to the boat.

They marched inside with Noah and his family, and God closed the door.

Slowly at first, then faster and harder, rain poured down for forty days and forty nights.

But Noah's big boat floated on the water...

...and everyone inside stayed safe and dry.

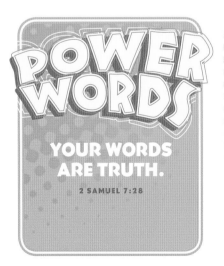

POWER WORDS

YOUR WORDS ARE TRUTH.

2 SAMUEL 7:28

ACTIVITY

Sing these words about Noah's big boat to the tune of "This Old Man":

Noah's boat, Noah's boat,
God kept Noah's boat afloat,
Just like he promised, and his words are always true.
I can trust God. So can you!

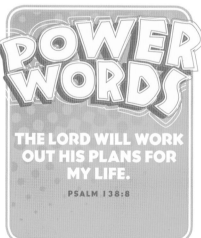

ACTIVITY

Find your backpack or ask a grown-up for a small suitcase. Pretend you are going with Abraham on his journey. Pack your backpack or suitcase for the trip. What will you take with you?

Jacob's Camping Adventure

GENESIS 28

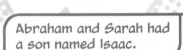

MIGHTY THOUGHT

God is always with us.

Abraham and Sarah had a son named Isaac.

After Isaac grew up and married Rebekah, they had twin sons, Esau and Jacob.

When Jacob grew up, he wanted to get married. He traveled to the land where his uncle lived to find a wife.

Good-bye!

He started the long walk to his uncle's house.

As the sun went down, Jacob found a good place to camp. Jacob yawned. He stretched. He found a rock for a pillow. He fell asleep and dreamed.

Jacob saw a stairway so tall it reached from earth to heaven. Angels climbed up and down the stairway, and God stood at the top. God said...

JACOB!

I promised this land to your grandfather Abraham and to your father, Isaac. My promise is for you, too. Your family will be a blessing to everyone on earth. I will watch over you wherever you go, and I will bring you back to this land.

Jacob woke up.

God is here, and I didn't know it!

In the morning, Jacob picked up his rock pillow.

THWACK!

He stood it on one end. It would always remind him of his dream and God's promise.

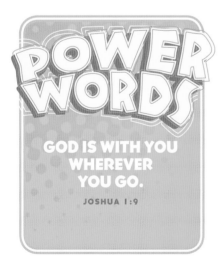

POWER WORDS

GOD IS WITH YOU WHEREVER YOU GO.

JOSHUA 1:9

ACTIVITY

Camp out in the backyard or somewhere inside your house. What will you use for a pillow?

Dream Teller

GENESIS 37; 39-46

MIGHTY THOUGHT

God makes bad things turn out for good.

Joseph's jealous brothers sold him as a slave.

Joseph worked for a man named Potiphar in Egypt, far away.

At Potiphar's house, Joseph got in trouble for something he didn't do.

Potiphar threw Joseph into prison.

The prison door locked. Joseph could not get out!

CLICK!

Two servants of the king were in prison too. They had dreams they couldn't understand. Joseph told them the meaning of their dreams.

One servant said...

When I get out of prison, I'll help you get out too.

But he forgot.

Later the king had a dream. Then the king's servant remembered Joseph. The king said...

Bring Joseph here!

Joseph told the king the meaning of his dream. In seven years, no crops would grow! People would be hungry. Joseph said...

You must store up grain now.

I will put you in charge!

When no crops grew, Joseph's brothers traveled to Egypt to buy grain. Joseph cried and hugged his brothers.

My brothers!

You sold me as a slave, but God brought me here to save your lives!

So Joseph's brothers and his father, Jacob, moved to Egypt, where there was food.

POWER WORDS

I WILL SEE THE LORD'S GOODNESS.

PSALM 27:13

ACTIVITY

Joseph hugged his brothers when he saw them again.
Give the people in your family a big hug today!

Trouble in Egypt

EXODUS 1 - 12

MIGHTY THOUGHT

God is always in charge.

Jacob's family grew bigger and bigger. The new king of Egypt was afraid.

Too many Israelites! They might try to take over. I will make them slaves.

He made the Israelites work day and night.

We need help!

God heard them. From a burning bush, God called...

Moses! Lead my people out of Egypt.

Moses went to see Pharaoh.

God wants his people to leave Egypt.

No! The people can't go!

So God sent trouble to the land of Egypt.

First the river turned red, and no one could drink from it. Then frogs hopped everywhere, even inside houses. Gnats covered everyone like dust.

Then flies swarmed through the air—everywhere except where the Israelites lived! Cattle got sick. People got painful sores on their skin. Hail hurt the crops, and grasshoppers ate what was left.

God kept the Israelites safe.

27

WHOOSH!

Darkness covered everything for the Egyptians, but the Israelites had light. Some Egyptians died, but God protected the Israelites.

Finally Pharaoh said...

Okay! You can go!

The happy Israelites hurried out of Egypt.

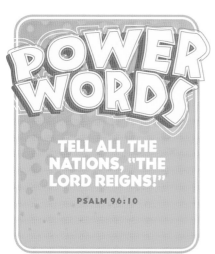

POWER WORDS

TELL ALL THE NATIONS, "THE LORD REIGNS!"

PSALM 96:10

ACTIVITY

In a dark room, put a blanket over chairs to make a tent. Turn on a big flashlight inside the tent. When God covered Egypt with darkness, he gave light to his people, the Israelites!

Walls of Water

EXODUS 14-15

MIGHTY THOUGHT

God is a mighty leader.

The people of Israel shook and cried. Behind them was Pharaoh's army. In front of them was the sea!

Moses said...

Don't be afraid! God will rescue you today. He will fight for you himself. Stay calm, and watch what happens.

A tall cloud moved between the people of Israel and Pharaoh's army. The people walked forward just as God had told them to.

29

Moses raised his walking stick over the sea.

God sent a strong wind. The wind blew a wide path through the sea. The people crossed the sea on dry ground between two walls of water!

Pharaoh's army chased the Israelites. But God made their chariots hard to drive. Pharaoh's army shouted...

Let's get out of here!

When all the Israelites had crossed the sea, Moses raised his walking stick again.

SWISH!

SWOOSH!

SPLASH!

The walls of water crashed down. Safe at last! The Israelites sang and danced, praising God.

POWER WORDS

LEAD ME IN THE RIGHT PATH, O LORD.

PSALM 5:8

ACTIVITY

Play Follow the Leader with a friend or grown-up. Take turns being the leader. Whatever the leader does, everyone else does too. Make funny faces, walk like an elephant, do somersaults in the backyard—just follow the leader!

Ten Good Rules

EXODUS 19-20

MIGHTY THOUGHT

God's rules are for our good.

God freed his people and led them into the wilderness. God said...

I love my people. If they will obey me, they will be my special treasure.

We will obey!

Moses said...

Get ready to worship! God will meet with you in three days.

On the morning of the third day, thunder crashed and lightning flashed! The people heard a long, loud blast on a ram's horn.

BWWAHHH!

Everyone trembled.

Moses led the people out of the camp.

They saw a mountain covered with smoke, and they knew God was there. The ram's horn blew again.

BWWAHHH!

The mountain shook.

Then Moses spoke, and God answered in the thunder. God called Moses to the top of the mountain.

The people watched Moses climb the mountain to meet with God.

God said...

Here are the rules my people must obey.

He gave Moses ten good rules, written on two large stones.

POWER WORDS

I LOVE YOUR COMMANDS MORE THAN GOLD.

PSALM 119:127

ACTIVITY

Gather some coins, pebbles, nuts, or pieces of wrapped candy. Count them by twos and then by tens.

STORY **10**

Can Donkeys Talk?

NUMBERS 22

MIGHTY THOUGHT

God wants us to obey him.

The king wrote a letter to Balaam.

Come and visit me. I have a job for you.

But God told Balaam not to go.

Balaam obeyed...at first. Then he changed his mind. He saddled up his donkey and started off to see the king.

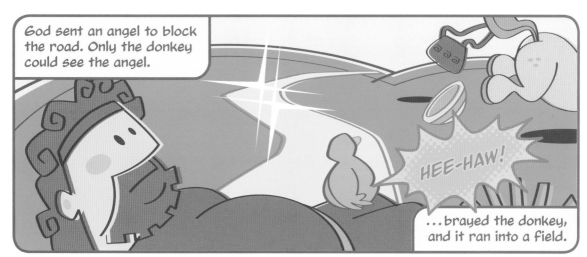

God sent an angel to block the road. Only the donkey could see the angel.

HEE-HAW!

...brayed the donkey, and it ran into a field.

Next the angel stood at a narrow place in the road between two vineyard walls. The donkey tried to squeeeeze around the angel. Balaam's foot scraped against the wall. Balaam still couldn't see the angel!

The angel moved farther down the road. The donkey stopped and plopped down in front of him.

Balaam yelled and hit the donkey. Then God let the donkey talk!

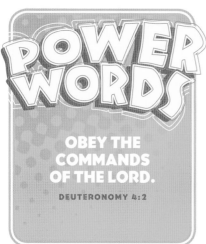

POWER WORDS

OBEY THE COMMANDS OF THE LORD.

DEUTERONOMY 4:2

ACTIVITY

Make a Put the Tail on the Donkey game. On a large sheet of paper, draw the side view of a donkey without a tail. Post the drawing on a wall. Use a feather or a piece of yarn for a tail. Attach tape to the tail. Now close your eyes and try to stick the tail on the donkey.

Rumble, Tumble!

JOSHUA 5-6

MIGHTY THOUGHT

God makes his power known.

Joshua, the new leader of Israel, stood outside the Israelites' camp. He saw Jericho, a city with tall stone walls. God wanted the Israelites to live in this land, but how would they get past those walls?

Joshua saw a man nearby. Who was this? Joshua asked...

Friend or enemy?

The man had a sword.

I'm in charge of the Lord's army.

I'm at your service! What should I do?

The Lord said...

Get your fighting men. March around Jericho once a day for six days. Seven priests must blow their horns. On the seventh day, march around Jericho seven times. Then shout! The walls of Jericho will fall down.

Joshua told the people...

Line up! March with me around the city walls. Don't talk. The priests will blow their horns, and the Lord will lead the way.

The people obeyed. Left, right. Left, right. Every day for six days, they marched around the tall stone walls of Jericho.

On the seventh day, the people marched around the city seven times. Then Joshua yelled, "Shout!" and all the people shouted.

RRRUMBLE!

TUMBLE!

The strong walls of Jericho came crashing down!

POWER WORDS

HE HAS SHOWN HIS GREAT POWER TO HIS PEOPLE.

PSALM 111:6

ACTIVITY

March around the room while you chant these words aloud. Or you can sing the words to the tune of "Ring around the Rosy." Be sure to fall down at the end like the walls of Jericho did!

Marching around Jericho,
Just the way God told us.
Rumble, tumble!
The walls fall down!

Kindness Counts

RUTH 1–4

MIGHTY THOUGHT

God rewards the good things we do.

Naomi told Ruth, her daughter-in-law...

I'm leaving Moab and going home to Bethlehem. My husband and my sons have died. You stay here and go back to your mother's house.

Ruth said...

I want to go with you and help you. Your God will be my God.

Ruth and Naomi walked together down miles of dusty roads.

In Bethlehem, Ruth picked up grain in a field. Bend and reach. Bend and reach. Ruth filled her basket with barley so Naomi could bake bread.

Boaz, the owner of the field, asked...

Who is that young woman?

She is Ruth, from the land of Moab.

Boaz told Ruth...

Stay here in my field. Gather all the grain you want. Drink water from our well.

Thank you, sir. I don't deserve such kindness.

You came here to help Naomi. You trusted God to care for you. May God reward you for what you have done.

Soon Boaz married Ruth. Ruth and Boaz had a baby boy! They named him Obed.

WAAA!

WAAA!

Naomi was a happy grandma now!

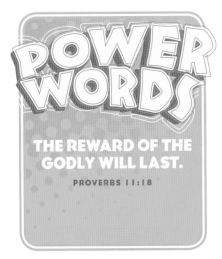

POWER WORDS

THE REWARD OF THE GODLY WILL LAST.

PROVERBS 11:18

ACTIVITY

Buy a box of quick-cooking barley. With help from a grown-up, grind the barley into flour in a blender. Use the barley flour to bake biscuits or bread, just like Naomi and Ruth did.

Who's Calling?

I SAMUEL 3

MIGHTY THOUGHT

God speaks to us.

Young Samuel helped Eli the priest at the big tent where people worshiped God.

At night Samuel slept in the tent to guard it.

One night when Samuel was sleeping, a voice called to him.

SAMUEL!

Samuel jumped up from his bed. He ran to Eli. Samuel asked...

Did you call me? Here I am. What do you need?

44

I didn't call you. Go back to bed.

The voice called again.

SAMUEL!

Here I am. Did you call me?

THUMP

THUMP THUMP

Samuel ran to Eli. Samuel asked again...

I didn't call you. Go back to bed.

SAMUEL!

THUMP THUMP

THUMP

Samuel ran to Eli.

Here I am. Did you call me?

It is God calling you. If you hear the voice again, say, "Speak, Lord. Your servant is listening."

SAMUEL!

Samuel sat up.

Speak, Lord. I'm listening.

God gave Samuel an important message. From then on, Samuel served the Lord.

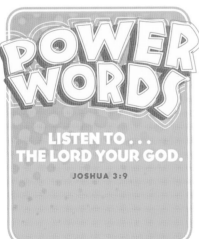

POWER WORDS

LISTEN TO . . . THE LORD YOUR GOD.

JOSHUA 3:9

ACTIVITY

Play a listening game. Sit outside or inside with a grown-up or a friend. Close your eyes. What are all the different sounds you can hear?

A Giant Surprise
I SAMUEL 17

MIGHTY THOUGHT

God rescues his people.

Nine-foot-tall Goliath stomped his giant-sized feet. He waved his giant-sized spear. He yelled at the Israelites...

Send someone over to fight me!

David asked...

Why is everyone afraid? Don't worry about Goliath. I will fight him.

Don't be silly. He's a giant. You're a boy.

...the king said.

I'm coming in the name of the Lord. Today everyone will see that God rescues his people, but not with sword and spear!

THUD

David put a stone in his sling and hurled it at Goliath. The stone hit Goliath in the head, and he fell down with a giant-sized thud.

God used David to rescue his people from their enemies!

POWER WORDS

OUR GOD IS A GOD WHO SAVES!

PSALM 68:20

ACTIVITY

Lie on the floor. Ask a grown-up to place books or blocks on the floor beside you from your heels to the top of your head. Measure the line. That's how tall you are. Then make another line of books or blocks nine feet long—that's how tall Goliath was!

Bird Food

1 KINGS 17

MIGHTY THOUGHT

God takes care of us.

God told his people not to worship idols. Bad King Ahab did anyway.

God sent Elijah to Ahab with a message. Elijah said...

There will be no dew or rain during the next few years until I give the word!

No rain meant no crops. No crops meant no food. Elijah's message made Ahab angry.

God told Elijah...

Hide from Ahab. Stay by the Kerith Brook. Drink from the brook. Eat what the ravens bring you. I have given them orders to bring food to you.

Elijah did what God said. He set up camp near the Kerith Brook. When he was thirsty, he drank from the brook.

Every morning he watched for the ravens.

Every evening he watched for the ravens.

They swooped into his campsite with pieces of bread and meat in their big beaks.

CAW!

CAW!

Bread and meat for Elijah to eat—just as God promised!

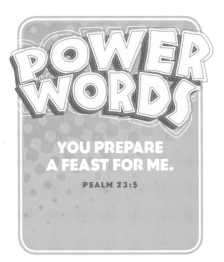

POWER WORDS

YOU PREPARE A FEAST FOR ME.

PSALM 23:5

ACTIVITY

Have an Elijah lunch or snack. Drink water, just like Elijah did. Ask a grown-up to cut a slice of bread into small pieces. Cut a slice of lunch meat into small pieces too. Pretend you are Elijah, eating the food the ravens brought.

Naaman's Decision

2 KINGS 5

MIGHTY THOUGHT

God heals our bodies.

Naaman, the army commander of Aram, had a terrible skin sickness. Who would help him?

A young girl said...

Naaman should go see Elisha, God's prophet in Israel.

So Naaman traveled to Israel with his horses, chariots, and army officers.

He went to Elisha's house.

Elisha sent a message out to Naaman:

Go wash yourself in the Jordan River seven times. Then God will heal you.

How silly! I'm too important to do that.

Naaman's officers said...

If it were a hard thing, you would do it. This is an easy thing.

Naaman wanted to get well. He decided to obey. He went to the Jordan River.

He bobbed in the muddy water seven times. And on the seventh time, Naaman's skin looked smooth and new.

Naaman went back to see Elisha. Naaman said...

Now I know there is no other God in all the world except the Lord!

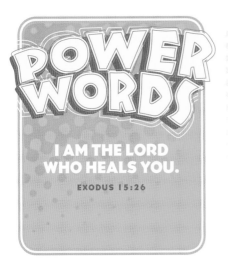

POWER WORDS

I AM THE LORD WHO HEALS YOU.

EXODUS 15:26

ACTIVITY

Go outside and fill a dishpan with water. Add some dirt to make the water muddy. Find an old doll or toy to bob up and down in the muddy water seven times, like Naaman did.

Lost and Found

2 CHRONICLES 34

MIGHTY THOUGHT

God's Word never changes.

Josiah was a good king. He said...

The Temple of God needs repair. Let's get to work!

Builders fixed the ceiling and put up new beams.

ZOOMFA ZOOMFA

They patched crumbling walls with new stones.

In the Temple, Hilkiah the priest found a scroll, a book on rolled-up paper. He wondered...

What's this?

AAACHOOO!

He brushed off the dust and dirt.

Then he said...

Moses wrote this long ago! These are God's words to us!

Hilkiah gave the scroll to King Josiah's secretary, who read it to the king. King Josiah cried...

I feel so sad! We and our parents and grandparents have not obeyed God's Word! We have not been doing what this scroll says we should do.

King Josiah called all the people to meet him at the Temple. He read the words on the scroll for everyone to hear.

We're glad to hear the words of God!

They promised to obey God from then on, and God brought peace to their land.

POWER WORDS

LORD, YOU ARE MINE! I PROMISE TO OBEY YOUR WORDS!

PSALM 119:57

ACTIVITY

Ask a grown-up to help you make a scroll. Find two unsharpened pencils, a sheet of paper, and some tape. Cut the width of the paper to one inch less than the length of the pencils. Turn the paper the long way. Tape one pencil to each end of the paper. Roll both pencils toward the middle of the paper. When your scroll is complete, unroll it and write on it Psalm 119:57 (the Power Words to the left).

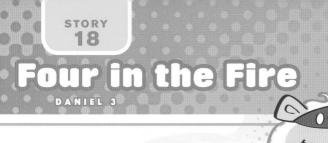

Four in the Fire

DANIEL 3

MIGHTY THOUGHT

God keeps us safe.

King Nebuchadnezzar made a tall golden statue. The king's messenger said...

When the music plays, everyone must bow down and worship the statue.

Horns tooted. Flutes fluted. Harps hummed. All the people bowed—except Shadrach, Meshach, and Abednego.

The king yelled...

Look! We put three men in the furnace, but now there are four!

God had sent help to Shadrach, Meshach, and Abednego. They were not burned one bit!

Praise to the God of Shadrach, Meshach, and Abednego! Only he can rescue like this!

The king told them to come out. Shadrach, Meshach, and Abednego came out. God had kept them safe. The king said...

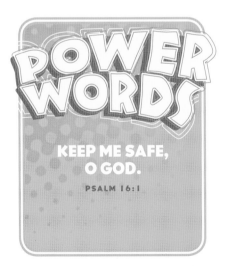

POWER WORDS

KEEP ME SAFE, O GOD.

PSALM 16:1

ACTIVITY

God worked a miracle for Shadrach, Meshach, and Abednego. But God keeps us safe from fire by helping us learn fire safety rules. Talk with a grown-up about fire safety. Help your family make a fire safety plan. aThen draw a picture of your plan.

Daniel for Dinner?

DANIEL 6

MIGHTY THOUGHT

God works mighty miracles.

The king of Babylon made a law that people could pray only to him. But Daniel loved God and prayed only to God.

Some of the king's helpers said...

Daniel won't obey the king's law! Throw him into the lions' den!

The king liked Daniel. The king told Daniel...

I am sorry about the law I made.

But the law was the law. The king's helpers picked Daniel up and threw him into the den of hungry lions. The king cried...

May your God rescue you!

THUD

That night the king could not eat or sleep. In the morning he hurried to the lions' den.

ACTIVITY

Get a paper plate, some yarn and glue, and crayons or markers. Draw the face of a lion on the paper plate. Add some yarn for the lion's mane. Ask a grown-up to print "God does mighty miracles" around the bottom of the plate. Put the lion in your room to remind you to pray to God, just like Daniel did.

Swimming with a Big Fish

JONAH 1-3

MIGHTY THOUGHT

God wants everyone to know him.

God told Jonah...

Go to Nineveh. Warn the people. Everything they do is bad.

Jonah didn't like the Ninevites. So Jonah ran the other way.

He found a ship, bought a ticket, and went on board.

NINEVEH

He thought he could get away from God.

Inside the fish, Jonah prayed...

Oh God, Please help me, and I will praise you. You are the only one who can save me.

After three days, God told the fish to spit Jonah out onto dry land.

BURP!

This time Jonah went to Nineveh and gave God's message to the king and the people. They listened. They asked God to forgive them for the wrong things they had done. They started doing what was right.

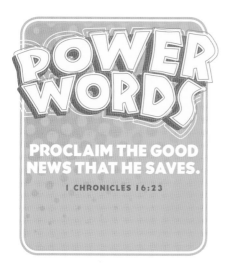

POWER WORDS

PROCLAIM THE GOOD NEWS THAT HE SAVES.

I CHRONICLES 16:23

ACTIVITY

Jonah needed a loud voice to give God's message to the people of Nineveh. Make a megaphone so your voice will be louder. Wash an empty plastic milk jug and let it dry. Ask a grown-up to carefully cut off the bottom. Decorate the milk jug using crayons, markers, stickers, or glue and colored paper. Then hold the handle with one hand and talk into the spout.

Big Night in a Little Town

LUKE 2

MIGHTY THOUGHT

God sent his Son.

Sheep snuggled, cozy and warm.

BAA BAA

CRACKLE HISS

A campfire sizzled.

ZZZ ZZZ

Sleepy shepherds guarded their sheep under the dark night sky.

Suddenly an angel appeared! Bright light surrounded the shepherds. The angel said...

Don't be afraid! I have good news for you and all people. God's Son, Jesus, has been born. He is the Savior! You will find him wrapped in strips of cloth and lying in a manger.

Then all the angels of heaven filled the sky. They sang...

Glory to God! Peace on earth!

The angels disappeared. Then the shepherds said...

Let's go! Let's find the baby the angel told us about.

In Bethlehem the shepherds found Mary and Joseph and the baby. Baby Jesus was wrapped in cloth and lying in a manger. The shepherds said...

It's him! Just like the angel told us!

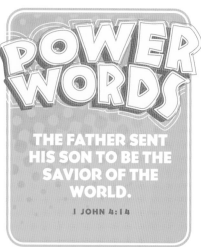

POWER WORDS

THE FATHER SENT HIS SON TO BE THE SAVIOR OF THE WORLD.

1 JOHN 4:14

ACTIVITY

Ask a grown-up to help you learn how to swaddle a baby. (You can use a baby doll.)

Pretend to be the shepherds worshiping baby Jesus in the stable. Sing this lullaby to the baby, to the tune of "Are You Sleeping?"

Baby Jesus, Baby Jesus,
God's dear Son, God's dear Son.
We are glad to see you!
We are glad to meet you!
Go to sleep, go to sleep.

70

Too Many Fish

LUKE 5

MIGHTY THOUGHT

Jesus leads us.

Jesus grew up. He began to preach and teach. One day he sat in Peter's boat and taught the people sitting on the beach. Jesus said...

Peter, let's go fishing. Take the boat out to deeper water. Let down your nets to catch some fish.

Peter said...

We fished all night. We didn't catch a thing. But if you say so, okay. I will do it.

Peter rowed the boat out to deeper water. He threw the heavy nets into the water. Down, down they went. Suddenly...

71

James and John rowed out to help. The fish filled up their boat too!

Where had all of the fish come from? Peter and the others looked at Jesus. Jesus said...

Don't be afraid. From now on you will be fishing for people. Come and follow me!

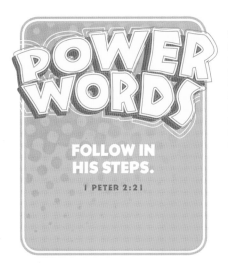

POWER WORDS

FOLLOW IN HIS STEPS.

1 PETER 2:21

ACTIVITY

Make footprint patterns, right and left, by tracing around a grown-up's shoes. You can use a crayon to trace the footprints on colored paper; then cut them out. Make a footprint trail around the house and follow it. Jesus wants us to follow him!

Through the Roof

MARK 2

MIGHTY THOUGHT

Jesus heals the sick.

A man who couldn't walk lay on a mat. Four friends carried him to see Jesus. The friends said...

Here's the house where Jesus is. Hold on. We're going in.

But they couldn't even get near the door. There were too many people!

CLOMP CLOMP CLOMP

Hold on! We're going up!

They carried the man up the stairs to the roof.

Jesus looked at the man.

My friend, stand up. Pick up your mat and go home!

The man stood up! He could run! He could jump!

We've never seen anything like this before!

He picked up his mat and walked through the crowd. Amazed, all the people praised God.

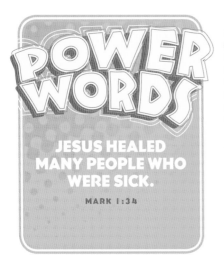

POWER WORDS

JESUS HEALED MANY PEOPLE WHO WERE SICK.

MARK 1:34

ACTIVITY

Do ten things that use your legs. Here are some ideas to get you started. Can you walk? run? jump? march? hop? skip? dance? stand on your tiptoes? ride a bike? climb a jungle gym? What else can you do?

Wind and Waves Obey Him

MARK 4

MIGHTY THOUGHT

Jesus' power can calm any storm.

Jesus told the disciples...

Let's cross over to the other side of the lake.

So Jesus and the disciples, his twelve special followers, all got into a boat.

Jesus said...

I'm tired. I need a nap.

A fierce storm came down on the lake. The wind blew hard and strong.

WHISH! WHOOSH!

SLAP! SLAM!

Huge waves crashed over the boat.

Jesus looked at his disciples.

Why were you afraid?

Jesus' disciples shook their heads. They had never known anyone like Jesus.

Even the wind and the waves obey him!

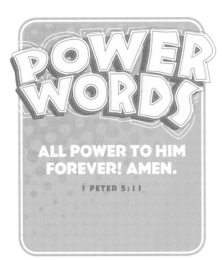

POWER WORDS

ALL POWER TO HIM FOREVER! AMEN.

1 PETER 5:11

ACTIVITY

Make a boat on the floor with cushions or use a big box. Sing these words to the tune of "Row, Row, Row Your Boat" as you pretend to row across the sea with Jesus.

Row, row, row your boat
on the stormy sea.
Jesus calmed the wind and waves
and he'll take care of me!

Feeding Hungry People

MARK 6

MIGHTY THOUGHT

Jesus gives us what we need.

The people listening to Jesus rubbed their hungry tummies. The disciples said...

RUMBLE

GRUMBLE

It's getting late. Let's send the people away so they can buy food.

Jesus said...

We don't have to send them away. You can feed them.

The disciples said...

But there are so many people! And we have only five loaves of bread and two small fish.

The bread and fish didn't even run out. Five thousand men and their families ate as much as they wanted. The five loaves of bread and two little fish fed a big crowd!

When everyone was full, the disciples gathered up the leftovers in twelve baskets.

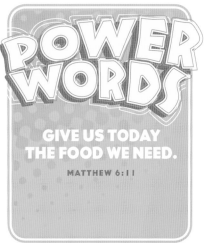

POWER WORDS

GIVE US TODAY THE FOOD WE NEED.

MATTHEW 6:11

ACTIVITY

What do you eat in a day? Make a picture list and find out. On a sheet of paper, draw pictures of everything you eat today. Thank God for giving you the food you need every day.

Busy Martha

LUKE 10

MIGHTY THOUGHT

Jesus teaches us.

Work, work, work! So much to do! Dinner for Jesus must be just right.

Sweep the floor. Set the table. Run to the market and home again. Start the oven. Roast the meat. Bake the bread.

BUBBLE

BUBBLE

Boil the vegetables! Hurry, hurry, hurry!

Suddenly Martha stopped. She wiped her forehead and pushed back her hair. She said...

Mary should be helping me.

Where was her sister, Mary?

Martha stepped out of the kitchen and looked around.

Jesus sat in the living room, teaching about God. Mary sat at his feet, listening to every word.

Jesus! This isn't fair! My sister just sits there while I do all the work! Tell her to come and help me.

Martha put her hands on her hips.

Jesus said...

My dear Martha, you are fussing about so many details! Only one thing is worth so much effort, and Mary has found it. It's listening to me.

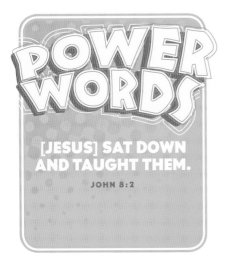

POWER WORDS

[JESUS] SAT DOWN AND TAUGHT THEM.

JOHN 8:2

ACTIVITY

God speaks to us through the Bible. Ask a grown-up if there's a red-letter Bible at your house. Or plan a visit to a bookstore and look at one there. Flip through some of the pages in Matthew, Mark, Luke, and John, and you can see all the words of Jesus printed in red ink! Wow! That's a lot of important words!

Lazarus, Come Out!

JOHN 11

MIGHTY THOUGHT

Jesus gives life!

Jesus came to the village of Bethany. His friend Lazarus had died. Martha and Mary said...

If you had been here, our brother would not have died.

Jesus asked...

Where have you put his body?

Come and see.

Mary and Martha and Lazarus's friends took Jesus to a cave shut tight with a large stone. Jesus cried.

Jesus said...

Move the stone away.

Lazarus walked out of the cave! He was alive again! Grave clothes were wrapped around his hands and feet, and a cloth covered his head.

Take off the grave clothes and let him go!

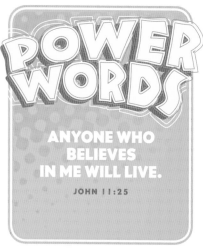

POWER WORDS

ANYONE WHO BELIEVES IN ME WILL LIVE.

JOHN 11:25

ACTIVITY

Sing these words to the tune of "Three Blind Mice."

Lazarus! Lazarus!

Come out now!

Come out now!

Jesus has power over everything!

Even dead people can rise and sing.

This is the reason that Jesus is King!

Thank you, God!

Thank you, God!

Never Too Busy

MATTHEW 19

MIGHTY THOUGHT

Jesus loves children.

Boys and girls skipped and hopped along the path. Babies squealed in their mothers' arms. Soon they would see Jesus!

There he is!

The disciples scolded the crowd.

STOP!

Don't go any farther.

A mother said...

Please, sir, we want to see Jesus. We want him to bless our children.

The disciples said...

Jesus is busy. He doesn't have time for children.

Jesus said to the disciples...

STOP! Let the children come to me. Never keep them away. I am not too busy for children. Children are important in my Kingdom. Everyone must enter my Kingdom with faith like a little child's.

The children smiled. The mothers and fathers smiled. The disciples stepped aside, and the children ran to Jesus.

He took them in his arms. He put his hands on their heads and blessed them. He held the babies and blessed them, too. Then he went on his way.

What a happy day!

POWER WORDS

LIVE . . .
AS CHILDREN
OF GOD.

PHILIPPIANS 2:15

ACTIVITY

A blessing is a special prayer you say when you're with the person being blessed. You can bless your brothers and sisters, friends, parents, or grandparents. Touch the person's head or shoulder and say, "May your love for God be strong. May you always follow him."

Parents and caregivers, you can bless your children too! Here's an example, adapted from Ephesians 1:15-20: "May you grow strong in faith, love, and wisdom, knowing God well. May your heart be full of his light. May you always experience the mighty power of God toward those who believe in Jesus Christ."

Short Man in a Tall Tree

LUKE 19

MIGHTY THOUGHT

Jesus came to save us.

Zacchaeus tried to squeeze through the crowd to see Jesus. No one would let the little man in.

Please let me through. I want to see Jesus too!

So Zacchaeus ran ahead and climbed a tree. And he was just in time, because Jesus was coming his way.

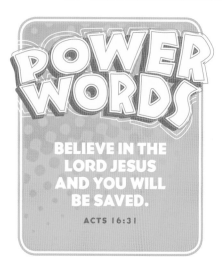

POWER WORDS

BELIEVE IN THE
LORD JESUS
AND YOU WILL
BE SAVED.

ACTS 16:31

ACTIVITY

Zacchaeus went looking for Jesus, and Jesus was looking for him! Play a game of hide-and-seek with a friend or a grown-up. Take turns pretending to be Zacchaeus and Jesus.

Parade for a King
MATTHEW 21

MIGHTY THOUGHT

Jesus is our King.

Jesus walked with his disciples toward the big city of Jerusalem for the Passover Feast.

CLIP-CLOP

CLIP-CLOP

Two disciples found a young donkey for Jesus to ride on. They threw their coats over the donkey's back. Then Jesus sat on it and rode toward the city.

People who were going to the city filled the road. People in the city heard that Jesus was coming. The people said...

Let's go out to meet him!

When the people saw Jesus, some spread their coats on the road. Some spread palm branches from the fields. Coats and branches made a colorful path for Jesus to ride on.

Jesus' followers surrounded him as he rode along. They sang and praised God with loud voices.

Praise God! Blessed is the King who comes in the name of the Lord!

The parade for Jesus came into Jerusalem. The whole city noticed. The people said...

Who is this?

This is Jesus, the King!

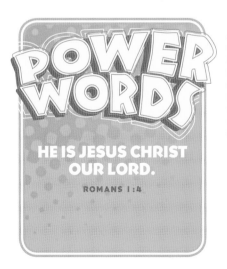

POWER WORDS

HE IS JESUS CHRIST OUR LORD.

ROMANS 1:4

ACTIVITY

Pretend you are going to Jerusalem with Jesus, and have a parade. Some friends can ride on riding toys. You might play rhythm instruments like drums and cymbals too. Sing a praise song as you parade around your house or neighborhood.

The Place of the Skull

MATTHEW 27; LUKE 23

MIGHTY THOUGHT

Jesus died for us.

Jesus' followers couldn't understand what was happening. On a hill called the Place of the Skull, soldiers nailed Jesus' feet and hands to a heavy wooden cross. But Jesus had never done anything wrong!

Jesus knew this was why he came to earth. God had planned for his own Son to be punished for the sins of the whole world. Jesus said...

Father, forgive them. These people don't know what they are doing.

At noon, the sky went dark. At three o'clock, Jesus called out to God, and then he died.

A man named Joseph took Jesus' body down from the cross. He wrapped it in linen cloths and laid it in a tomb in a rocky place. He closed up the tomb with a big stone.

The soldiers guarded the tomb. Jesus had said that after he died, he would rise again on the third day! But some people didn't believe him and didn't want anyone to steal Jesus' body.

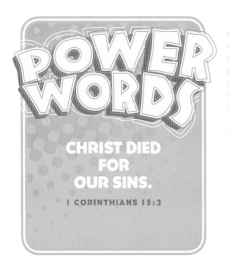

POWER WORDS

CHRIST DIED FOR OUR SINS.

I CORINTHIANS 15:3

ACTIVITY

Jesus never did even one wrong thing. But he died for the wrong things we do so we can live with him in heaven forever. Find two Popsicle sticks or two paint stirrers. Write "JESUS" across one stick and "SAVES" down the other. Glue the sticks together like a cross, with the "S" in the middle of "JESUS" overlapping the "S" at the beginning of "SAVES."

Rumble! Zap! Pow!

MATTHEW 28

MIGHTY THOUGHT

Jesus is alive!

Early on Sunday morning, just as the sun began to shine, two women went to visit Jesus' tomb.

They felt so sad because Jesus was dead.

Suddenly a big earthquake shook the ground.

RUMBLE!

An angel came down from heaven, rolled away the stone, and sat on it.

ZAP!

The guards outside the tomb fainted!

The angel spoke to the women.

Don't be afraid. I know you are looking for Jesus. He isn't here! He has risen from the dead, just as he said! Come, see the place where his body was lying.

The women peeked inside the tomb. It was empty!

POW!

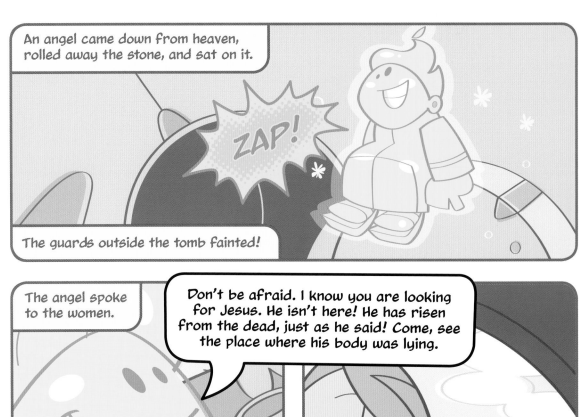

The angel said...

Now go quickly and tell his disciples the news!

Don't be afraid. Go and tell my disciples to meet me in Galilee. I will see them there.

The women turned and ran with joyful hearts. On the way, they saw Jesus! They ran to him and worshiped him. Jesus said...

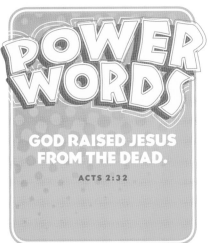

POWER WORDS

GOD RAISED JESUS FROM THE DEAD.

ACTS 2:32

ACTIVITY

Easter is a special time to celebrate that Jesus is alive again. Flowers, colored eggs, baby chicks, and bunnies help us think about new life. But we can celebrate Easter and new life all year long.

Plant some peas or beans in your yard or in a container. Be sure to water the seeds and make sure they have plenty of sunshine. Then watch them grow! From just a little seed comes a brand-new plant.

Breakfast on the Beach

JOHN 21

MIGHTY THOUGHT

Jesus forgives us.

On the night before Jesus died, Peter had acted like he didn't know Jesus—three different times!

He felt bad about what he had done.

Peter said...

I'm going fishing.

Some of the disciples went with Peter. They fished all night, but they didn't catch any fish.

In the morning, they saw a man standing on the shore. He said...

Throw in your nets to the right of the boat.

So they did and the nets filled up with fish!

Jesus looked at Peter.

Peter, do you love me?

Jesus asked this question three times. Three times Peter answered...

You know I do, Lord.

Then Jesus said...

Feed my sheep and follow me!

Jesus had work for Peter to do! Peter knew he was forgiven.

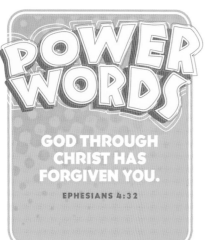

POWER WORDS

GOD THROUGH CHRIST HAS FORGIVEN YOU.

EPHESIANS 4:32

ACTIVITY

Have a backyard breakfast of bread and fish sticks with your family. How do you think Peter felt when Jesus forgave him? Talk about what forgiveness means to you.

Ride on a Cloud

ACTS 1

MIGHTY THOUGHT

Jesus will come back.

Forty days after he came back to life, Jesus led his disciples to the Mount of Olives. Soon he would leave his friends and return to heaven. Jesus said...

Wait in the city for the Holy Spirit to come. You will receive power. Then tell people everywhere about me.

As Jesus prayed for his disciples, a cloud surrounded him and carried him up to heaven.

107

The disciples worshiped Jesus. They would miss him, but their hearts beat joyfully just the same.

THUMP THUMP

THUMP THUMP

THUMP THUMP

They went back to Jerusalem and waited, just as Jesus had told them to do.

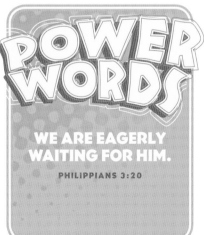

WE ARE EAGERLY WAITING FOR HIM.

PHILIPPIANS 3:20

ACTIVITY

Play a cloud-watching game with a friend or a grown-up. Go outside and look up at the clouds. Lie on your back if you can. Find clouds with shapes that look like something else. Take turns. Say, "I spy a cloud that looks like _ _ _ _ _ . Can you find it?"

The Holy Spirit Comes

ACTS 2

MIGHTY THOUGHT

Jesus gives us power to live for him.

After Jesus went back to heaven, his disciples stayed together in a house. When they were all together in one room, suddenly a sound like a mighty windstorm filled the room.

ROAR!

WHOOSH!

Flames of fire danced above each person's head. God had sent the Holy Spirit!

FLICKER!

FLUTTER!

The Spirit filled all the people who believed in Jesus. They began to speak in languages they didn't even know.

People from many places around the world lived in the city. They heard the noise and rushed to see what was happening.

How can this be? These people from Galilee are talking in our languages. We can understand what they are saying!

Peter stepped up and told the crowd the Good News about Jesus.

Jesus is alive again! God has sent the Holy Spirit. If you turn away from your sins and turn to Jesus, you can be forgiven and have the Holy Spirit too. This is God's promise to all people everywhere.

About three thousand people believed what Peter said and were baptized that day.

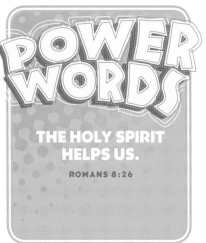

POWER WORDS

THE HOLY SPIRIT HELPS US.

ROMANS 8:26

ACTIVITY

Do some push-ups, sit-ups, and jumping jacks. Exercise makes our bodies strong. The Holy Spirit makes our spirits strong and helps us do what's right. Thank God for the power of his Holy Spirit.

Walking and Leaping

ACTS 3

MIGHTY THOUGHT

We can do mighty things in Jesus' name.

Every day a man sat beside the Temple gate. He was a lame man—he could not walk.

Please could you help me?

He hoped the people going to the Temple would give him some money.

One afternoon Peter and John went to the Temple. The man saw them as they walked his way. The man asked...

Please could you help me?

Peter said...

Look at us!

The man held up his hand, expecting money. But no coins *plink-plinked* into his cup.

The man jumped up. He stood! He walked! Then he went into the Temple with Peter and John—walking, leaping, and praising God!

HALLELUJAH!

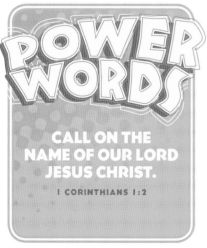

ACTIVITY

Say a cheer for Jesus. You can learn this cheer or make up one of your own. You can also make up motions to go with the words.

Jesus, Jesus, he's the best!
He is stronger than the rest!
When we call on Jesus' name,
We will never be the same!
J . . . E . . . S-U-S! Jesus!

Paul's Big Surprise

ACTS 9

MIGHTY THOUGHT

Jesus gives us new life.

Paul had a goal: find Christians and hurt them! He didn't believe in Jesus.

But on the road to Damascus, Paul got a big surprise.

116

A light from heaven shone around Paul. He fell to the ground. Then he heard a voice.

Paul, why are you hurting me?

BAM!

Paul asked...

Who are you?

I am Jesus. Get up and go into the city now. You will be told what you must do.

Paul stood up. He couldn't see! His friends led him into the city. He stayed there for three days. He was still blind! He didn't eat or drink.

A man named Ananias came to see Paul. Ananias said...

The Lord Jesus sent me here. He wants you to have your sight back.

Then Paul could see again!

He was baptized right away.

Now Paul was a Christian! He had a new life—teaching and preaching about Jesus wherever he went.

POWER WORDS

NOW YOU HAVE NEW LIFE.

ROMANS 6:13

ACTIVITY

What would it feel like to be blind? Ask a grown-up to cover your eyes with a scarf and then lead you around the house. Do you know where you are? How do you feel? Talk about how Paul felt when he couldn't see.

Peter's chains fell off. The guards kept sleeping.

The angel said...

Get dressed! Put on your shoes!

Now put on your coat and follow me.

Peter did what he was told. The guards snored on.

CRRREAK!

Peter thought he was dreaming. He followed the angel down the hall. None of the guards saw him! The big iron gate opened by itself. Peter walked outside with the angel. They started down the street, and suddenly the angel disappeared.

Peter said...

I'm not dreaming! God sent an angel to set me free!

He hurried to find the Christians who had been praying for him.

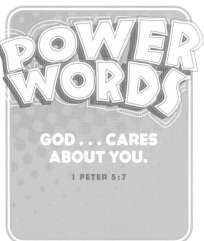

POWER WORDS

GOD . . . CARES ABOUT YOU.

I PETER 5:7

ACTIVITY

Make paper chains with strips of construction paper and tape or glue. Wrap the chains around your feet and wrists, and ask someone to fasten them so they won't fall off. Then pretend to be Peter in prison when the angel appeared. Take off your chains and let them fall right off!

Shipwreck

ACTS 27-28

MIGHTY THOUGHT

God gives us courage.

Paul went to Rome on a big sailing ship. On the way, the ship ran into a terrible storm. Wind, waves, and rain hid the sun and the stars.

The sailors gave up hope. Paul told them...

Have courage! God is taking care of us. He sent an angel to me last night. The angel said we will all live. But we will be shipwrecked on an island.

Finally the ship neared land. Paul encouraged the sailors to eat. They hadn't eaten anything for a long time. Paul said...

You have been so worried. Please eat now for your own good.

The sailors tried to sail to the land, but waves hit the ship and broke it to pieces.

SMASH!

Some sailors swam toward the land. Others floated on boards from the ship. Everyone reached land safely.

The people on the island welcomed the sailors with a big bonfire. Paul stayed on the island until spring.

CRACKLE!

POP!

Then he set sail for Rome on a different ship.

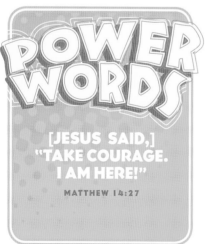

POWER WORDS

[JESUS SAID,] "TAKE COURAGE. I AM HERE!"

MATTHEW 14:27

ACTIVITY

When is a time that you need courage? When you get a shot at the doctor's office? When you want to be a friend to someone no one else likes? When you want to cheat at a game, but you know that would be wrong? Ask God for courage. Act out with a grown-up some of the ways you will show your courage.

Great Day!

I THESSALONIANS 4; REVELATION 21-22

MIGHTY THOUGHT

We have a forever home with Jesus.

God gave John a wonderful peek at the beautiful home in heaven we will live in someday.

The city shines like a sparkling jewel because God is there. Everything in the city is made of gold as clear as glass. Around the city stands a tall wall with twelve gates. Each gate is a single pearl.

The river of the water of life flows through the city from the thrones of God and Jesus. The tree of life is there too, with twelve different kinds of fruit.

There is no sun and no moon, no day and no night. Jesus gives the city light. God will live with us in the city. We will be his people, and he will be our God. There will be no sadness or crying. Everything will be new!

At the right time, Jesus will come from heaven on the clouds, with a loud shout and the sound of a trumpet!

BLAST!

Everyone will see him! Everyone who loves him will rise up to meet him in the air. Jesus will take us to our new home in heaven. What a great day that will be!

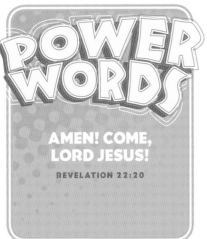

POWER WORDS

AMEN! COME, LORD JESUS!

REVELATION 22:20

ACTIVITY

Draw a picture of what you imagine heaven will look like. Decorate your picture with glitter, sequins, or shiny stickers. Heaven will be a beautiful place!

ABOUT THE AUTHOR & ILLUSTRATOR

DIANE STORTZ owns Izzy's Office in Cincinnati, Ohio, where she writes and edits for both children and adults. She has written almost fifty titles, including rhyming rebus books, board books, picture books, and first concept and counting books.

Diane clearly remembers the moment in first grade reading circle when reading "clicked" for her. She wants children everywhere to learn to love to read God's Word as much as she does today.

Diane and her husband, Ed, are the parents of two married daughters and have one grandchild, Solomon.

LUKE DAAB Ever since Luke Daab was little, he has enjoyed comic books and superheroes—Superman, Batman, and Aquaman being some of his favorites. aAs Luke grew older, he began to see how superheroes are like Jesus. They stand for truth, justice, honor, and sacrifice, and they always choose the right thing. Working on *Rumble! Zap! Pow!* has fulfilled one of Luke's dreams—to illustrate the stories of the world's greatest hero, Jesus.

Luke studied art at the University of Michigan and now operates a graphic design and illustration studio called Daab Creative. Luke is married to Jenny, and they live in a suburb of Chicago.